Little People, BIG DREAMS
COCO CHANEL

Little People, **BIG DREAMS**
COCO CHANEL

Written by
Mª Isabel Sánchez Vegara

Illustrated by
Ana Albero

Translated by Emma Martinez

Frances Lincoln
Children's Books

This is the story of a French girl called Gabrielle. When she was little, Gabrielle lived in an orphanage.

The nuns thought Gabrielle was very strange.
She was different and they didn't like it.

CHICKE

Gabrielle *was* different. While the other girls played, she liked to sew with a needle and thread.

When Gabrielle grew up, she sewed by day and sang by night.

The people watching called her "Coco."

When Coco finally went to bed, she dreamt in shapes and patterns. She wanted to make so many things!

One day, Coco made a hat for her friend.
Simple and elegant, it was different to the usual style.

Coco made more and more hats, until she had enough to open a hat shop. Her modern designs surprised the *mademoiselles* in Paris.

One evening at a party, Coco saw that the other ladies weren't dancing. Their corsets were too tight and they could hardly breathe!

So Coco created a brand new style, simple and straight. Her dresses and skirts would be comfortable to wear.

At her first fashion show, some people sneered.
Coco's clothes were too strange and different for them.

But as time went on, Coco showed them that to be stylish you don't need to wear corsets or sparkly sequins. . . .

. . . and being different might make other people think differently, too. That's why everyone now remembers the young Gabrielle as the great designer, Coco Chanel.

COCO CHANEL

(Born 1883 • Died 1971)

1932

1936

Coco Chanel was one of the most famous fashion designers that ever lived. She was born as Gabrielle Chanel in a charity hospital and grew up in a rundown house in a French town. Following the death of her mother, when Gabrielle was 11 years old she was sent to a strict convent school, where she learnt to sew. After school, she became a seamstress, sewing for a tailor during the day, while in the evenings she sang on stage. It was at this time that she earned the nickname "Coco" from the soldiers in the audience.

1937

1962

In 1908 she became a hat-maker and soon afterward opened her first shop in Paris. Soon she had more shops and started to sell clothes as well as hats. Her simple, elegant designs —which were straighter and shorter than normal, and freed women from corsets—took the world by storm. In 1918 Chanel opened a couture house in 31 Rue Cambon and three years later she unveiled her first perfume, Chanel No 5. She became a worldwide fashion icon and her comfortable, easy-to-wear styles changed women's clothes forever.

Want to find out more about **Coco Chanel**?
Have a read of these great books:

Different Like Coco by Elizabeth Matthews
Coco Chanel: Famous Fashion Designers by Dennis Abrams
Chanel Fashion Review: Paper Dolls by Tom Tierney
If you're in New York, you could even visit the Metropolitan Museum of Art,
where you can see some of Coco's famous outfits!
www.metmuseum.org

Text copyright © 2014 by Mª Isabel Sánchez Vegara
Illustrations copyright © 2014 by Ana Albero

First published in Spain in 2014 under the title *Pequeña & Grande Coco Chanel*
by Alba Editorial, s.l.u.
Baixada de Sant Miquel, 1, 08002 Barcelona
www.albaeditorial.es

First published in the USA in 2016 by Frances Lincoln Children's Books,
an imprint of Quarto Inc.,
276 Fifth Avenue, Suite 206, New York, NY 10001
www.franceslincoln.com

ISBN: 978-1-84780-784-7

Printed in China

1 3 5 7 9 8 6 4 2

Photographic acknowledgments (pages 28-29, from left to right) 1. French fashion designer Gabrielle 'Coco' Chanel (1883 - 1971) at a
London hotel, 1932 © Keystone Pictures USA / Alamy 2. Coco Chanel, French couturier. Paris, 1936 LIP-283 © Lipnitzki/Roger Viollet/Getty
Images 3. Photo © Pictorial Press Ltd / Alamy 4. Photo © Keystone Pictures USA / Alamy

Also in the *Little People,* **BIG DREAMS** series:

FRIDA KAHLO

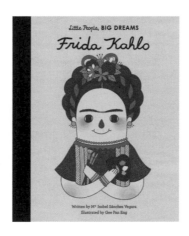

ISBN: 978-1-84780-783-0

When Frida Kahlo was a teenager, a terrible road accident changed her life forever. Unable to walk, she began painting from her bed. Her self-portraits, which show her pain and grief but also her passion for life and instinct for survival, have made her one of the most famous artists of the twentieth century. This inspiring story of her life features a facts and photos section at the back.

Discover the lives of outstanding people, from designers and artists to scientists. All of them achieved incredible things, yet each began life as a child with a dream.

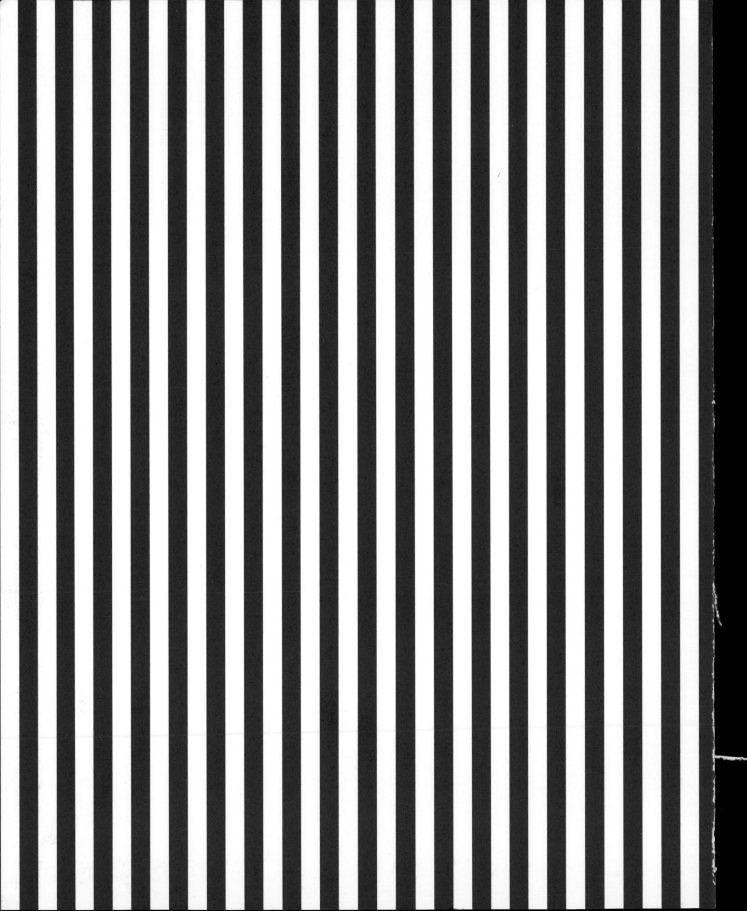